GOD'S REST AND REFLECTION!

DAY 7

Papa & Mama Goose

GOD'S REST AND REFLECTION! – DAY 7

Papa & Mama Goose

Copyright © 2020
Enchanted Rose Publishing
P.O. Box 991
Hempstead, TX 77445

Published by Enchanted Rose Publishing
Layout by Cynthia D. Johnson @
www.diverseskillscenter.com

Written by Papa & Mama Goose

Printed in the United States of America
ISBN-13: 978-1-947799-67-7

After looking at all that was created, GOD rested from making anything else.

He looked at the heavens, earth, and all their hosts.

Before rain ever appeared, GOD created the first irrigation system to water the ground.

Then, he formed a man from the dust to take care of the Garden of Eden, man's home.

GOD also place the Tree of the Knowledge of Good and Evil in the middle of the garden.

GOD obviously had a discussion with the man regarding the Tree of Knowledge.

GOD commanded Adam not to
eat of its fruit.

It appears that Adam earnestly took GOD for His word.

Adam seemed to have understood that by eating of the forbidden tree, there would be dire consequences.

Neither was there any indication that Adam desired the fruit or wanted to be a god.

Adam seemed focused on work and maintaining his relationship with GOD.

GOD and Adam's relationship appeared to be solid before anyone else came along.

Here is a teachable moment...some relationships can even take us away from the presence of GOD.

As Adam interacted with the animals, he surely observed that every animal had a mate.

But, Adam had no representation of his kind.

Perhaps Adam felt lonely.

It wasn't as if he could have a heart-to-heart with a cheetah.

He certainly could

not make a replica

of himself.

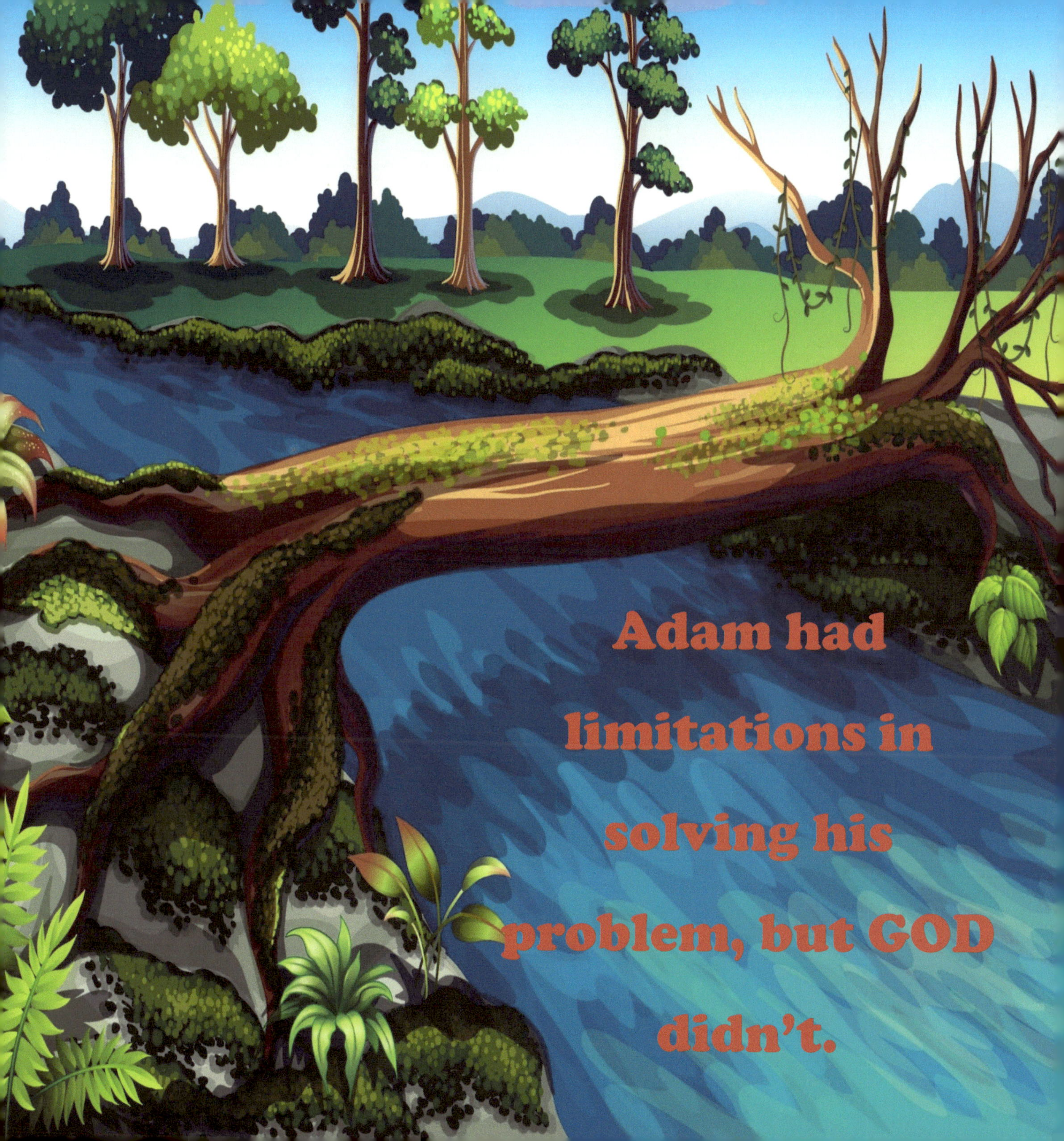

Adam had limitations in solving his problem, but GOD didn't.

GOD could see into the future and knew that Adam would need a companion to help him through the challenges that would later come.

So, GOD caused Adam to fall into a deep sleep and took one of his ribs from his side, then closed it.

From Adam's
rib, GOD created
a mate suitable
for him.

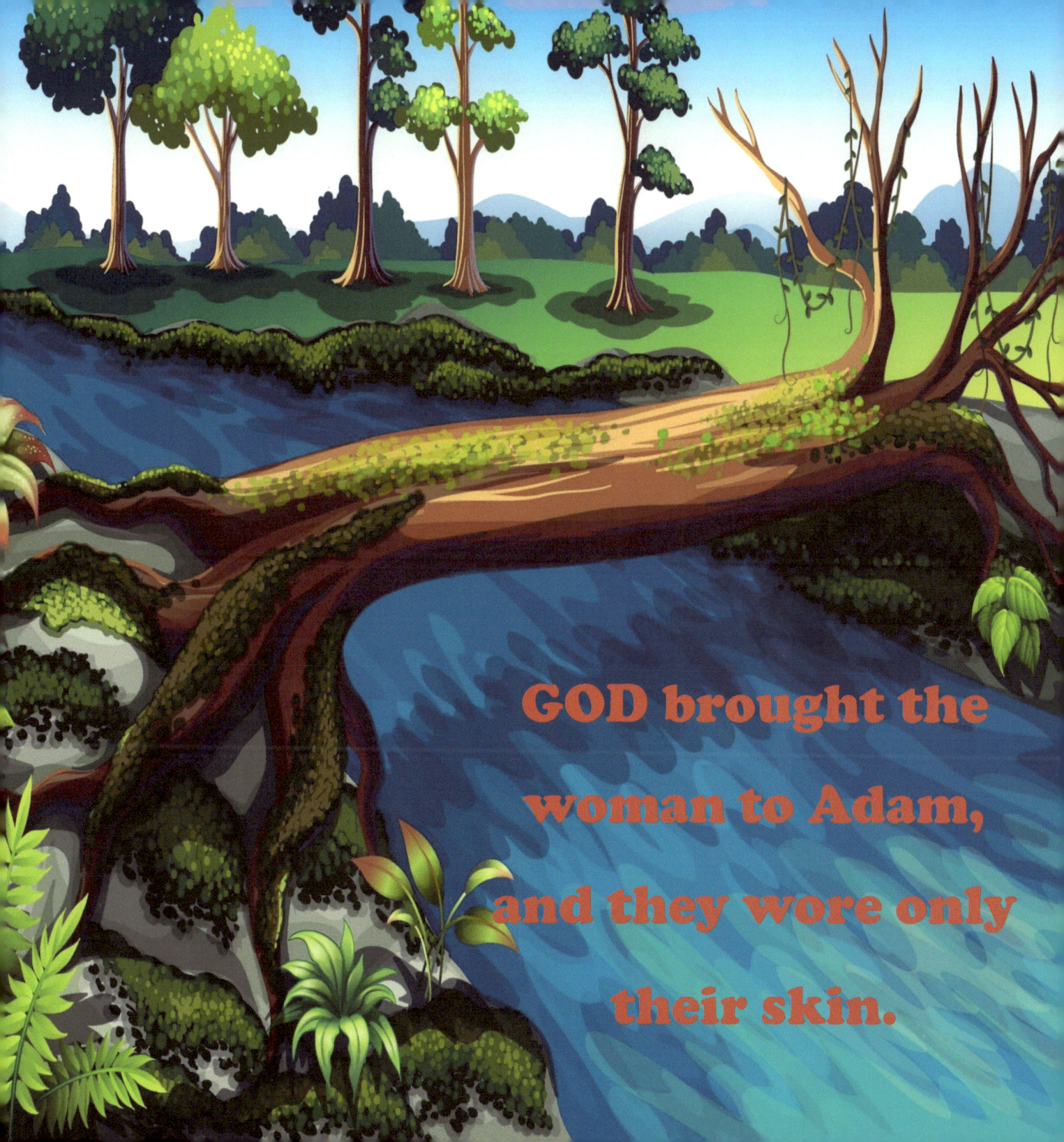

GOD brought the
woman to Adam,
and they wore only
their skin.

I imagine the woman was the most beautiful of all the creatures Adam had laid eyes on.

Adam called his mate, woman because she was made from a part of him.

Now, GOD would allow Adam to be the leader of his own household.

Thus, GOD performed the first wedding ceremony, giving Eve away to Adam.

This is the blueprint GOD created for marriage.

The institution of marriage was a spiritual and physical union between a Man and a Woman.

It is an abomination to see how Satan has twisted the gender roles of marriage in society.

One thing is certain...No matter what people do or say, GOD's word will Never Pass Away!

GOD'S REST AND REFLECTION! – DAY 7

Written by Papa & Mama Goose

Copyright 2020

by

Mama Goose Books

Hempstead, Texas

Papa & Mama Goose Media

Through the power of their faith and instructions from GOD's HOLY SPIRIT, these humble servants of CHRIST take us back to our beginning...The Bible. Although Papa and Mama Goose have written a plethora of books, none can hold a candle to how the WORD of GOD has guided their lives. Realizing that life on Earth is temporal, Papa and Mama Goose wanted to write Books about the Bible that would provide a Biblical Foundation for young children. The goal of the books is to teach youngsters to know and fall deeply in Love with GOD.

It was during their years in college that Papa and Mama Goose found CHRIST. They were taught the Gospel and baptized into the Prairie View CHURCH of CHRIST at Prairie View A & M University in Prairie View, Texas. Papa and Mama Goose enjoy sharing the same spiritual birthday. Currently, the dynamic duo are faithful members of the Fifth Ward CHURCH of CHRIST in Houston, Texas.

Follow Me On...

 Facebook
www.facebook.com/goma
magoose

 Twitter

@GoMamaGoose

 Instagram
MamaGoose Paris
gomamagoose@gmail.com

www.ingramcontent.com/pod-product-compliance
Lightning Source LLC
Chambersburg PA
CBHW041238040426
42445CB00004B/70